C000152443

PERFECT
MADNESS

*Escaping the confines of conformity,
making the impossible possible and
redefining the road to success in your life!*

ALASTAIR MACARTNEY

VOLUME 1

All rights reserved. No part of this book may be reproduced in any form without permission in writing from the author. Reviewers may quote brief passages in reviews.

Published by Perfect Madness Publishing

ISBN-13: 978-0692311165
ISBN-10: 0692311165

Disclaimer

No part of this publication may be reproduced or transmitted in any form or by any means, mechanical or electronic, including photocopying or recording, or by any information storage and retrieval system, or transmitted by email without permission in writing from the publisher. While all attempts have been made to verify the information provided in this publication, neither the author nor the publisher assumes any responsibility for errors, omissions, or contrary interpretations of the subject matter herein. This book is for entertainment purposes only. The views expressed are those of the author alone, and should not be taken as expert instruction or commands. The reader is responsible for his or her own actions. Adherence to all applicable laws and regulations, including international, federal, state, and local governing professional licensing, business practices, advertising, and all other aspects of doing business in the US, Canada, UK or any other jurisdiction is the sole responsibility of the purchaser or reader. Neither the author nor the publisher assumes any responsibility or liability whatsoever on the behalf of the purchaser or reader of these materials. Any perceived slight of any individual or organization is purely unintentional.

No Warranties: The authors and publishers don't guarantee or warrant the quality, accuracy, completeness, timeliness, appropriateness or suitability of the information in this book, or of any product or services referenced by this book. The information in this book is provided on an "as is" basis and the authors and publishers make no representations or warranties of any kind with respect to this information. This book may contain inaccuracies, typographical errors, or other errors.

Liability Disclaimer: The publishers, authors, and any other parties involved in the creation, production, provision of information, or delivery of this book specifically disclaim any responsibility, and shall not be liable for any damages, claims, injuries, losses, liabilities, costs or obligations including any direct, indirect, special, incidental, or consequential damages (collectively known as "Damages") whatsoever and howsoever caused, arising out of, or in connection with, the use or misuse of the site and the information contained within it, whether such Damages arise in contract, tort, negligence, equity, statute law, or by way of any other legal theory.

Copyright © 2014 Alastair Macartney
All rights reserved

Your Free Gift

I know that there are lots of different books that you could have purchased instead of this one. As a way of saying thank you for choosing this book to purchase I am giving away a free Toolkit. This Perfect Madness Toolkit provides you with everything you will need to a live in the Perfect Madness frame of mind and is exclusive to my book and blog readers.

The journey that you are planning to embark on is not easy. Opening your mind to all the possibilities in the world can be exhausting. However, to ease your transition to an enlightened free spirit, I have carved many small steps into the mountain you will climb and provided a handrail as you navigate your new path.

You can download this toolkit directly by going here: http://www.PerfectMadness.com/Toolkit

Table of Contents

Introduction

$\mathcal{I}$ haven't always lived life with a Perfect Madness mindset. To begin with, I didn't know any better. To begin with, I tried to fit in as part of the pack. I was the sheep or the lemming that followed everyone else. I followed them because that's what everyone else did. It's what was expected of me. Or at least, it's what I thought was expected of me. I lived within the confines of conformity.

The change didn't happen suddenly. I'd always had a slightly mischievous streak. I think I got it from my father and I think he got it from his father. I'm sure my unborn son will get it from me.

My father used to tell me so many stories as I was growing up. There was excitement and adventure, danger and accomplishment, challenging the status quo and yet succeeding. These were real stories that he'd lived himself. To me, they were incredible feats.

I wanted the same. I wanted just a fraction of this excitement. I wanted more than this excitement. I wanted any of this excitement that I could possibly get.

The good news is that I've been on an amazing journey. Along the way I've met members of the Royal family and city Mayors, been arrested on terrorism charges, jailed and deprived of my liberties in a solitary confinement cell, accused of being a spy and, believe it or not, I've been hunted down and outed in the National media for being a UFO.

The bad news is that it didn't happen overnight. I look back now and much of what my father had achieved seemed impossible to me. How could a scrawny, spotty boy like me even get close to attempting such feats? Even worse, what if I was able to try and I then failed? How could I possibly go on if that was the case? Perhaps it would be better for me not to try. If I didn't try then I couldn't possibly fail. Who was I to succeed?

I put my dreams to one side and followed convention. Well, I mostly followed convention. There were times when I deviated a little, more though on a limited basis and on selected occasions. I'd do something different. I'd follow a different path, I'd go against the norm. Sometimes it didn't work; I'd fail. But, sometimes I'd be successful and I'd achieve.

When I failed, I got back up, brushed myself down and carried on. When I was successful I built on my success. I realized that sometimes I achieved when I thought I would fail. My accomplishments were small but the victories were large. I made possible what I previously thought was, to me, impossible.

Over time I gained confidence in what I was doing. I continued to fail. But I would learn from my mistakes. I failed less and took on more. When somebody told me that I couldn't do something, or that it was impossible, I didn't take their answer as refusal of permission, I took their answer as a challenge.

Like many of us, I had incredible fears. Fears that I didn't think I would be able to overcome. Conquering my fears, making that impossible possible, was something that I really did think I would fail at. Somehow I persevered. I achieved. I believed in myself.

I learned that you can escape the confines of conformity, that many things that are seemingly impossible can be made possible and that the road to success is not measured in monetary value but in the value that I choose to use to define it. I discovered that life is what I chose to make it. It takes courage and commitment but by choosing to live my life in the way that I want to, not following the definition of others, or my perception of their definition, I can create a happy, more exciting and more energizing life. It really is Perfect Madness.

Earlier this year my wife and I received the fantastic news that she was pregnant with our first child. Amongst the tears of joy and celebratory toasts, I wondered how this would affect my Perfect Madness life. Would I now need to settle down, grow up and conform? Would my definition of success now need to be based around working in an office cubicle and bringing in enough money to look after my family? It would be remiss of me not to have done a personal audit and evaluated my life. I concluded it quickly.

Life shouldn't change. My values, my personality, my beliefs will all stay the same. It's who I am and what I believe. As I've journeyed along a slightly unpredictable life with highs and lows, accomplishments, success and failures, I've discovered so much that I want to pass on. My critical thinking and analysis has revealed an array of incredible life lessons. These are lessons I wish I had known. They are lessons I must share with my son-to-be.

As I put pen to paper (actually fingers to keyboard) I realized that these lessons shouldn't just stay private. There was value for all. Documenting these lessons in a book for you the reader and, when he's old enough, my currently unborn son. There are lessons for every one of us. And that is how this book began.

I'm not perfect by any means and my life and existence has bounced against a variety of imperfections. I've battled and struggled in places, like most of us have. But I've often gone against the grain, done things in a different way and yet achieved what others have failed to even dare.

I've leapt from the KL Tower in Malaysia setting a World Record, led a team of human flight specialists to fly a wingsuit formation from the infamous north face of the Eiger and past a line known as the Murderous Wall; and I became World Champion by winning the ProBASE World Cup Istanbul Showdown. I've traveled the world, including places like Hong Kong, Croatia, Thailand, New Zealand, Singapore and Afghanistan. I have a unique and happy marriage with my soul mate, have an eclectic group of incredible friends and, despite my skepticism towards it, I've found comfort in the practice of yoga and, more recently, meditation.

My secrets, my life lessons, are contained in this book. Some of them you might know already, others you might just need a gentle reminder of and some may be totally new. We are all different and we will all need to find the little tips, tricks and lessons that work specifically for us.

Making This Book Work For You

This book is organized into seven key chapters and each chapter containers a number of lessons. Each lesson and each chapter can stand on its own. You can pick out the parts that work for you and skip any parts that don't. Read the book your way.

It's often easier to read a book from start to finish. I have purposely kept this book short. Each chapter can easily be consumed in one sitting. My suggestion is to read this book one chapter at a time and take in the information. That can be from start to finish or in any order that you choose. Make notes and highlight the parts that interest you. Refer back to these again.

Take action and implement. Don't be one of the people that read a book, like the ideas but never put them in to practice. Commit to applying one lesson from each chapter before you start the next chapter. It doesn't need to be anything big. But do something. By starting, by doing, you're more likely to continue and eventually develop a habit.

Redefining Possible

Our world, the one we see with our own eyes and listen to with our own ears, is made up of our experiences. This is largely defined through our upbringing. As we develop in life we permit additional influence from a broader range of external stimuli. Yet, often, how we process those stimuli is based on the grounding we already have. We might watch and hear but it can be very difficult to truly and independently see and listen. The differences are extremely subtle yet extremely large.

Possible and impossible aren't always the strict definition of what we can and can't do. They are also what the mind will or won't permit. Opening the door to your mind is a harder job than many might actually realize. I hope that this chapter might help you to glimpse through that door and help you to see and listen more to the world around you.

Normal Is For Freaks

What is normal? Is it the office worker that spends their 9-5 working day in a cubicle, an hour commute each way and with just a few weeks of vacation a year? Spending their free hours with their eyes plastered to the television, bum firmly planted on the sofa, watching other people live their lives? Is that what normal has become?

Who is the freak? The person with the long hair, with the Mohawk, with the facial piercings, with the tattoos? Or the individual who doesn't hold down a steady job but travels and lives life to the full?

I spent years looking at men with earrings and thinking they were losers in life. Honestly. My views of normal and abnormal were that established in my brain that these snap judgments weren't just easy, they came naturally. Then something strange happened - one became my friend. Slowly, I started to realize that the people I had ostracized from my life, the 'freaks' often had significant value to add and weren't so different after all.

I spent years in an office job, relentlessly turning up day after day to sit at my desk in a shared workspace, tapping away at the computer. I knew that this was how life was; I got a decent salary and would eventually move up the ladder until retirement.

But then I spent more time with the people that often had less money in their bank account than me. The people that many saw as 'social outsiders'; that I had seen as 'freaks'. I started to realize that it wasn't about what they had in their bank account but the true value was in the experiences they gained. Their true bank accounts, their memory banks, were crammed high with adventures and experiences, with life events and huge doses of unapologetic fun.

If you're that person who currently conforms to what is generally accepted as normal, looking at the other side and laughing, just remember, they are looking back at you and laughing harder. Consider your normal.

Disrupt

Disruption has become a buzzword in the entrepreneurial world, and particularly amongst tech businesses and start-ups. The concept isn't new but our technology enabled lives make disruption an increasing possibility with accelerated results.

Technically there is a difference between disruptive innovation and technological innovation but I don't plan to split hairs here. The cause doesn't matter, it's the principle of stepping outside of known possibilities. Challenging. Questioning. Defying convention. Asking why. Taking risk.

To disrupt will encompass the risk of failure. It won't always work. There will be traditionalists who hate what you're doing and what you stand for. There will be businesses that will stand to lose millions if you're right and if you're successful. There will be huge obstacles that will stand in your way.

Most likely you'll fail. At least at the beginning. But, if you've got what it takes and your idea is sound, you'll get back up, brush yourself off and make it happen.

You'll have supporters who will back you, encourage you and, perhaps, finance you. You'll break through, innovate and succeed.

When you're successful the haters will still be there (read more about haters in Chapter 5). While many will change their tune, wanting to befriend you and jump on your bandwagon to get a piece of the action themselves, the jealous crowd will remain, putting you down at every opportunity. It won't be easy. The people you meet in this world are like plants in a garden. You need to cultivate relationships with the beautiful flowers that radiate, support and enhance your life as they bloom. Simultaneously, you need to prune the weeds that suck you in and only try to bring you down with jealousy or selfish intentions.

No matter how innovative something is, there can always be more innovation. As cultural norms, requirements and generational changes happen, convention changes. Those that don't see this and don't constantly strive for improvement will be left behind.

The world as we know it wasn't created, and hasn't developed, to what it is now by people sitting back and accepting the current limitations as they are. People stood up to be counted. They innovated. They disrupted. You can too.

Black And White

Our world is full of black and white. There are rights and wrongs, ups and downs, justices and injustices. Some we agree with, others we don't. We debate and, sometimes, we compromise.

Compromise. In a world of black and white, where often we have to pick a side, to be on one side of the fence or the other, the word compromise is an interesting concept. Perhaps there's another option?

Our own personal experiences, upbringing and culture can cloud our judgments. Whether we like it or not we will approach everything from a preconceived intellectual position. If we were able to remove this subconscious stigma and think independently we might realize that what was once black and white, a clear yes or no, true or false, might not be. Perhaps there is a third answer.

Perhaps there might be more than just a third answer, a fourth or a fifth. And what are the effects of this third answer; the second and third order effects.

How do you know if there's a third answer? Perhaps you never will, but if you don't consider it you'll never know. Try:

** **The friend or colleague.** Find a friend or colleague that you can discuss this with and ask their viewpoint. The more different this friend or colleague is to you the better; they'll be more likely to consider it from a different position.

** **The parental approach.** Imagine you are your parents. Put yourself in their shoes. What would they think, how would then consider it.

** **The offspring.** What would your son or daughter think? It doesn't matter if you have a son or daughter or not, imagine it. However, if you do, ask them. Children can have both a remarkable clarity on the world and have an ingeniously creative imagination.

** **Being wrong.** Imagine you're wrong. Explore the possibility. Play Devil's Advocate. Argue against yourself and see what transpires.

There might well be truth to an argument, the answer could be no and the color could be black. It also might be none of those things unless you open your mind to the possibility and further consideration. Give it a go – you might surprise yourself with what you discover.

Be Weird

Weird is just plain weird. Weird can also be a little less weird. In fact, weird is what you chose to make it; weird is OK.

I've always been a little bit weird. I've been a little bit different. Special. Nothing hugely outrageous (in my opinion at least!), but just small twinges or limited doses of weirdness. When my friends were growing their hair long, I cut mine short. When they cut their hair short I wanted to grow mine long. When my peers came up with a plan I'd come up with different one that they hadn't even considered – often they didn't like it, but that's OK.

In life, I'd often look at others as weird. The punk rockers, the geeks, the bodybuilders, the transsexuals, the hippies, the travelers, the left wing, the right wing, the drug takers. They were the people that were different to me, different to my peers and to my values that I perceived at the time. To me, they were weird.

But then I started to change. Slowly, without realizing it, I became friends with each type of person on that list. It turns out that under their skin they were all good people. Sure, we all have our own weirdness but I suddenly realized that people could be geeks, transsexuals, hippies or do any other outrageously weird thing and actually, as human beings, could be good people.

I realized that weird wasn't weird at all. Weird was just a box that others, like me, put people into that they didn't understand. Weird was suddenly OK.

Then I realized that weird was cool. Cool because once you accepted that it was OK to be weird, whether in an extreme way or just in your own small personal way, you could be you. No hiding was required. You could be who you wanted to be without the worry of what other people might think. You could put your own brand on your life and live it as you intend to live it, not confined to the reality that you feel convention imposes upon you.

Everyone has their own little unconventional quirks. The quirks that make you, you. The quirks that help to define you. Don't hide behind them. Acknowledge them. Allow you to be you. Being weird isn't just OK, being weird is you. Don't live your life inside someone else's convention, live your life with all your individual traits that define your persona. Be you. Be weird.

Be Lucky

Luck is great. Some of us have it. Some of us don't. Are you one of the lucky ones, or one of those people that always miss out? One of those unfortunate people that, if something bad is going to happen, it's going to happen to you?

If you're one of the unlucky, you're now in luck. You might find this hard to believe but I can categorically say that you create your own luck. It's true. Let me give you some examples:

** Have you ever got to a train station and just missed your train?

** Had someone driven into the back of you, despite it not being your fault?

** Been caught out in the rain without your jacket?

All of these things could be down to bad luck. But here's what the lucky do – they create opportunities for success rather than letting divine intervention intervene for them. The reality – divine intervention isn't always on your side. You need to take control and take ownership of your own personal luck and direct it in the right direction.

When you're catching a train, the lucky person makes sure you leave enough time to get there early. They then add ten minutes. They give themselves a buffer. The unlucky person curses the traffic on the way to the train station, has no buffer and gets there as the train pulls away.

When driving, the lucky person looks in the rear view mirror and knows if the car behind is too close. They take account of this and give themselves extra braking distance to compensate and ensure harsh braking isn't necessary. The unlucky person is too busy rushing and is a little too close to the car in front. They manage to brake in time but the car behind doesn't. The accident might not be their fault, technically, but they have still been involved in an accident.

When heading out, the lucky person checks the weather forecast. They take their jacket if there's a chance of rain. They're prepared. The unlucky person takes a chance that, despite the forecast it might not rain and then wonders why they've been caught out without their jacket.

You can create your own luck or hide behind it. The choice is yours. Create it. Choose it. Be lucky.

Listen To Your Gut

There's something deep within you. Science can't explain it properly. It often defies logic. It often defies rational thought. Sometimes you have no idea where it comes from.

Your gut feeling is a survival mechanism. I know this from the very fact that I'm alive. I've listened to it when I've potentially been in situations where an error could cost me my life. Logic might have told me one thing but my gut, another. I chose to say no and follow my gut. Would it all have worked out if I hadn't followed my gut? Maybe. Maybe not. But I do know that, by following my gut instincts, it definitely did work out. Following your gut, reacting to that instinct and instructing yourself to follow its decision is one of the most powerful permissions you can authorize yourself to undertake.

In the last couple of decades the understanding of how the brain works has increased significantly. But, at the same time, if you ask any neurologist, they'll tell you that they are still amazed with the new things they learn and with how much they still don't know. The brain is a vastly complex organ and, certainly in our life times, we will never fully understand it.

We're all victims or our own experiences. These experiences help us in stressful situations when the adrenaline surges and we enter into the survivalist fight or flight mode. They also form the basis for our gut reactions in moments that are of a less stressful nature. Listen to your gut. That feeling is there for a reason.

Sometimes, our experiences cloud our judgment – we're not always right. Our gut can, on occasion, make the wrong call. This is where, intuitively, you need to hone that gut feeling. As you listen to it more, on smaller issues, you can tune in its accuracy. You can find when it makes the right call, when it makes mistakes and when it makes the wrong call. The more you let yourself use it, the more you will understand it. You'll be able to hone it, provide more feedback and top up your guts' experience bank. Your gut will develop and your intuition will be honed accordingly.

There might still be areas where your gut continues to under perform. Perhaps you have a particular fear or traumatic experience that prevents your gut from providing you with the right response. This is where your honing of your gut experience comes in to play. You take this to a second level. The first level is the initial gut response. With practice you can develop a second level of gut instinct; it's the analysis and gut-reaction of the initial gut-reaction. You can judge when the gut reaction is wrong and when you need to over-power or over-turn that reaction. You can learn to know when that reaction is wrong. This level of gut instinct takes time to develop but, as you learn to develop it, it can be incredibly useful and provide a basis to make incredible decisions.

Hone your gut. Let yourself succumb to the feelings that your body instinctively produces. Learn it. Allow it to make mistakes. Top up your experience bank and develop that second level gut reaction that will really provide intelligent instinct.

Developing Your Future

The future, your future, your tomorrow, is thoroughly in your hands. You create it. Your actions and decisions now will define it. What you do, what you choose, will have an impact.

The future you decide to live is not a future your parents have chosen. It's not a future that societal norms impose. It's not a future confined by conformity, limited by possibility or restricted by a false definition of success. It's a future defined by you.

As you educate yourself or others, recognize how much you do or don't know, restrict yourself within perceived boundaries or cross lines that perhaps you shouldn't, know that this is all within your control.

Take control and live your life, not anyone else's. Develop the future that you decide.

Learn For Tomorrow

We go to school to learn. As kids we don't have a choice. As adults we do.

We're always learning. We will never know everything. No matter who we are, how intelligent we are, how analytical we are, our brains just do not have the capacity to know everything about a certain subject. You might be the World's leading expert in a certain area but what you know about that subject is still extremely limited. New information is always on the horizon and opinions and theories are constantly evolving.

Over the last couple of centuries schools have developed significantly. From obligatory attendance and one room schools to what we see today. Yet this development has stalled. Children are now learning for today, or even yesterday. Often, they're not learning for tomorrow.

Education programs are educating for the jobs that existed five years ago or the jobs that exist today. They're failing to educate for the jobs and the opportunities that exist for tomorrow, in five years time and in twenty years time.

How will we communicate? Will we really need to be able to manually process complex arithmetic or should we focus on analyzing and understanding the big data that these equations produce?

If you're currently in an educational program then ask your teacher how the information they're presenting will benefit you in the future. If they don't know or can't answer then perhaps you're learning the wrong subject.

If you're a teacher and you're now questioning the relevance of your subject matter then it's time to take a stand. Without people standing up within their own educational institutions and forcing future-facing development there is little hope of unifying this necessary change. Gone are the days of studying a subject just because it's on the curriculum.

But what should we be learning for the future? The truth is, none of us know. If I did I'd certainly be a very rich man. For all of us it will be slightly different. Where do you see yourself in five, ten, twenty or fifty years? Most likely we'll need skills that analyze rather than compute. As we retreat into a more virtual environment, communication will become more critical. Speech and the written word will be more crucial but must be linked into a variety of learning styles to fully convey messages in a clear and concise manner. Cultural understanding and language will be key as we develop increased globalization. These are just a few ideas – some may be right, others wrong – but it's a start. The point is that our education systems need to at least have their eye on the future and take it into account when developing curriculum. Without this there is little hope for the radical change that is needed.

Don't just learn a subject because that's what everyone else is doing. Learn relevant skills that you can apply in the future, not skills you can only apply today.

The Knowledge Protocol

When things take a turn for the worse, they can take a turn for the worse very quickly. While errors don't happen often, when they do there is usually an element of human error somewhere in the chain of events. Many people far cleverer than me have spent many years researching and examining human error and ways to reduce it. In fact, a whole industry has been established.

Yet, despite the significant investment in reducing human error, we still make mistakes. So how then, can we reduce these errors to minimal levels?

As I have continued to push my own personal boundaries and step outside of my own comfort zone in the world's most dangerous sports, this is a question I have been continually asking myself. The answer, of course, is to remove the human element. Clearly though, this is not always an acceptable compromise.

If we are to continue to be involved, and to do so for the long term, then we need to adopt a long-term attitude. We need to work on the psychological aspects and on how we internally think about and perceive what it is that we do.

As I focused harder on my own personal risk mitigation strategies, I started to realize how much I knew. In doing so, I realized that in the big scheme of things how little that really was. As this evolved I developed The Knowledge Protocol. It's a philosophy that I use across all walks of life.

Although the Knowledge Protocol was developed in relation to my flying, it is now my philosophy, my theory and my approach to life. It took a while for me to understand it and even longer before I could deflate my over-inflated ego and start to apply it. To this day, **I still don't always get it right**, but by just *trying* to apply it is a large step in the right direction.

The Knowledge Protocol is:

"It's not about how much you know. It's about how much you don't know."

When you approach something, even if you're good at it, start considering how much you don't know about it rather than being over-confident and assuming how much of an expert you are. Even if you're the best of the best, do you really know everything there is to know on that subject? What have you missed? What else could you be missing? Think laterally.

The Knowledge Protocol is a mind set shift. It's about how you approach what you're about to do with an open mind.

We all like to think we're good at something. It strokes our ego. We all have an ego whether we choose to admit it or not. Some are much, much larger than others, but we all have them. What I'm asking you to do is turn the other cheek to that ego and step forward. I'm not saying forget it all together - having the confidence that goes with that ego can be healthy.

For many, I don't expect that to be easy. Others will believe they're capable of this but will pay lip service to it. But are the "cool kids", really the ones that show and tell everyone how great they are? Or are they, perhaps, the ones that are courageous enough to highlight their faults, errors and mistakes in an effort to improve further?

Start questioning.

Don't approach your next house purchase or your next car journey with the attitude that you know all about it. Start approaching it by questioning how much you don't know. You'll probably surprise yourself. There's so much information out there.

You don't need to do this on your own. Ask others for help. I love bouncing ideas off people that have different thought processes and levels of expertise to me. Find people that will take a different perspective or that have a different background. If you're strong enough, and this is more difficult than it sounds, throw your pride out the window. Ask someone with less experience for his or her advice. If you're an instructor, ask one of your students. Their point of view will be totally different from yours and they're likely to be considering different factors - factors that you might need to be considering too.

Take the challenge. Put that ego on hold. Throw pride out the window. Step out of your comfort zone. Challenge yourself. Apply the Knowledge Protocol. **It's not about how much you know. It's about how much you don't know.**

Don't Grow Up; It's A Trap

As a child we're encouraged to run around, play, smile, laugh, make mistakes, trip over, fall, get up again, fall. As we grow up we keep making mistakes but the smiles diminish. As a child, a small trip-up can be funny, later in life we develop a frown.

All of a sudden, life becomes more serious. Failure is not an option. We might become more determined to succeed but we take more sorrow in our struggles. Before we know it we've finished school and we're moving on to college and getting a job. It's a tough economy and job hunting is hard. It's easy to become trapped in a job that we didn't really want doing something that we don't really enjoy. In a flash ten years will have gone by, the ten years of the prime time of your life, where you've sat in a cubicle helping someone else make money but coming back with little satisfaction, little financial compensation and, perhaps most importantly, little enjoyment.

Remember those days as a kid when you'd smile? Those days where you made mistakes and it was OK and no one scolded you. Those days when you did what you want, unaware that there was a crowd to follow, unaware that there were expectations placed upon you.

Growing-up is a trap. Growing-up in a traditional sense means conforming to societal norms that inevitably remove a proportion of happiness from our lives.

Remember Peter Pan, the fictional boy who can fly and never grows-up? But have you heard of *puer aetemus*? It's Latin for *eternal boy* and used in Roman and Greek mythology to denote a child-god who is forever young.

Puer aetemus leads a life that questions authority, promotes freedom, pushes boundaries and overcomes perceived limits. *Puer aetemus* smiles.

Just because everyone else leaves school to start a life of 9-5 slavery, it doesn't mean you have to. Many won't have the courage to do anything different, and that's OK. But, for the few that dare to question this societal conformity and dare to stray from the herd, perhaps there is another option.

But what else is there to do? If you struggle to answer this question yourself then perhaps societal norms are the right place for you. Despite your wildest dreams perhaps a life as Peter Pan is for someone else.

Cubicle life is just one option. For those that can see and recognize this then you're already on the path to enlightenment. The universe is full of infinite options and limitless opportunities.

Every day more possibilities arise and more dreams are fulfilled. The Peter Pans, the puer aetemus' of this world seize these opportunities. You can too. Commit. Conquer. Achieve.

There's a Peter Pan in every one of us. He's waiting to break out. The question is, will you let him?

Dream To Create Memories

"It's the possibility of having a dream come true that makes life interesting." Paulo Coelho

Dreaming can be a phenomenal experience. There is countless research surrounding the benefits of sleep, our dreams, the types of dreams, the meanings of these dreams; the list goes on.

Dreaming is incredible. We can have a variety of dreams but right now I'm focusing on a specific type of dream. I'm not talking about the outrageous dreams involving science fiction and the impossible impossible. I'm talking about the dreams that we want to create, where we want to go, what we want to see, do, become. Traveling, career, goals, accomplishments. These might be what we see as impossible dreams – dreams that remain within the realms of reality but, to us, seem impossible. Not the impossible impossible but the possible impossible.

Dream these dreams. They might be small dreams, they might be large dreams. Perhaps it's to walk bare-footed in the sand holding hands with the most amazing person in the world. Perhaps it's to fly. Dream these dreams with intensity, passion, color, vigor.

Now live these dreams.

Create the dream you want to live. Dream it to create memories. Then take these dreams, these intentionally false imprinted projections and live them. Live the dream you create. You can choose to live it if you want it badly enough. These possible impossibles are achievable. They're achievable for each and every one of us if you want it badly enough.

You can find the person of your dreams. You can learn the skills and develop the technology and resources to achieve human flight. These are all possibilities that exist within your mind and can be transferred into reality.

Don't create excuses to hold you back. Follow the dreams. Create them as reality. Dream the most incredible dreams. Then live them.

Win Or Lose

Winning. It's important. No one likes to be a loser. Sometimes we get quick wins. They make us feel good. Sometimes our win takes a while – we need to invest a great deal of time and energy, work hard and battle for it. Sometimes it doesn't all go to plan. We lose.

We want to win. For most of us it's in our blood. We do what it takes to win. But what it takes can sometimes cross a line. Will you cross that line?

At some point you'll be tempted. You might only plan to step over that line briefly. Will the end justify the means? If you're veering close to that line and feel the magnetic draw across, then pause. Consider:

** How important is this win for you?
** Is it really worth compromising your values for this win?
** Is compromising your integrity really worth it?
** What are the long term affects effects of crossing this line and are you willing to take the risk?
** What are the long term effects of staying on the right side of the line despite the fact it could mean you lose on this occasion?

By pausing and asking yourself these questions it will help you step back and see. Often, when we're deeply embroiled in something we become too immersed to see clearly. Asking yourself these five questions will help you step back, just briefly, and provide you with an opportunity to understand the value of your win versus the value of crossing the line.

This won't give you all the answers. It won't make things crystal clear. But, by questioning if crossing the line is the right thing to do, it should give you that steer in the right direction.

If you want to be in this game for the long term you need to know that everyone gets caught out at some point. Sail close to it be all means, but, if you frequently cross the line, people will know. Each time you do it you're rolling the dice. How you play the game is more important than if you win or lose.

Be in it for the long term, not just the win. Stay on the right side of the line.

Belief

$\mathcal{B}$elieving in who we are and what we do is integral to the person we are now and the person we want to become. That means we need to indulge in our passions and believe in our own journey; the journey that we choose and that we create.

Happiness is integral to a successful and enjoyable journey. We need to take control and smile. We need to be honest with ourselves and with others.

If you want to reach for the stars, you can. Commit to it and achieve.

Life isn't worth living unless you indulge your passions

Of course, that's not strictly true - life is always worth living. But, how much joy will you really get out of life if you don't indulge your passions? Sure, you'll laugh with your friends and smile from ear-to-ear with your family. You'll cry when times are tough and get goose bumps when you go on that first date with someone incredibly special. Throughout all of that, have you really lived? When you're sat in that retirement home looking back on your life, treasuring your memories, will you be able to say that you've really, deeply indulged your passions or will you see a life of missed opportunities? A life of following the same predictable path as everyone else does?

Passions are within you for a reason. Seek them out. Engage them. Feel them. Embrace them. You might not know it at the time but your passions are there, guiding you. They're making you stronger, they're making you richer. Not just your wallet either, but your experiences, and your sense of self-worth. They're there to take you to a place that only your subconscious knows exists. Your mind is far more powerful than you can ever know. It has figured out your passions for a reason and it's going to use these passions to take you on the most incredibly exhilarating journey, far beyond your wildest dreams. But, only if you let it.

Sure, it's a risk. You'll lose some conscious control as you provide authority to your subconscious prefrontal cortex. And this brain lobe won't always get things right; as it engages its execution function it will need to learn to work with this new authority that you have now delegated to it. But accept mistakes, allow error and failure – it's a fantastic way to learn. These short-term failures will create long-term opportunities. It might not feel like it at the time but, trust me, it will add value to your longer-term life.

Stand strong and have the courage to indulge in your passions. Don't let the naysayers bring you down or prevent you from straying from the herd, from being an individual. Sure, listen to their advice but then make your own judgment. Passions are there for a reason – indulge them.

Live with Integrity

Life can be tough. We all get dealt some particularly powerful blows at times. Often, they are when we least expect it or at times when we think life couldn't get any worse.

When life has knocked you down, it can be especially easy to make compromises, the wrong compromises, and take the easy way out. At these times, when we've probably already dropped our guard lower than we should allow, we have to be even stronger.

That's why we need to maintain our honor and integrity, why we need to stand strong and remember who we are and our place in the community and not bow to external pressures.

Car insurance firms provide a bad example of those pressures. Too often they tell us not to apologize if we have a crash, whether we're in the right or the wrong. These firms fear the implication that apologizing could be conceived as an admission of guilt and potential litigation may ensue. Yet, in telling us to refuse to apologize, especially if we are in the wrong, they are removing our ability to be honorable humans. If we're wrong, one of the most fundamental aspects of humanity is not only for us to accept our mistake and apologize, but for us to attempt to right the wrong we have committed. It is a human right, and the honorable thing to do.

Living with integrity isn't about getting things right all the time; that would be living without being human. We all make mistakes. But it's about correcting those mistakes; making the next move a step in the morally right direction even if it seems the more difficult route to follow, rather than continuing to spiral down the path of least resistance. It also means apologizing when we're wrong and then taking the next step to do something about it and right those wrongs. That's what counts. That's what living with integrity is about. That's what humanity is about. That's what will make you a stronger and more respected person.

Reach For The Stars

On a clear night have you laid down on the cool grass, gazing up at the stars above? Have you wondered what it would be like up there, dreaming about it?

Perhaps you have a different dream. Or many dreams. Perhaps it's something simpler. Perhaps you want to start your own business, complete a half marathon or learn a new language.

Whatever the dream, the goal, the ambition, don't be put off by how far away it might be. Don't be put off by how unachievable it may seem. Don't listen to the negative-minded individuals who tell you it can't be done or that you can't do it. And don't listen to your inner voice when it tells you that you're going to fail.

If you want it badly enough, if you really want it, it'll happen. You'll find a way. You'll overcome the obstacles. You'll defeat adversity. You'll prove them all wrong.

But, you have to believe. You have to defeat the voices both around you and in your own head which say you're going to fail, even when times are tough. If you can do this, you'll achieve. Be fueled by the naysayers; regard them as a challenge. Go on a mission to prove them all wrong. Set the goal in your mind as a factual point in your future, then identify all that stands in your way, tackling each obstacle one at a time. The road to completion may take months, years, decades, but the length of the journey only serves to harden your resolve, strengthen your character and ultimately sweeten the reward.

As you lie looking up at the stars at night, believe you can be there. Don't throttle back your ambition but allow it to manifest into something as large as the galaxies above.

Take Responsibility

Your actions, what you do, how you perform, your decisions in life, the people you hurt, the people you love, how you feel, your choices, they are all down to you. No one else. Only You.

You have a choice. You can influence the outcome. You can choose to say no. You can choose not to be in that situation in the first place. It might have been a long line of events which brought you to where you are, but, win or lose, you chose to be there. In doing so, you chose to live with the outcomes.

Most of the time those outcomes will positive. You can take credit for those outcomes while thanking and appreciating those who helped you along that journey. But, there'll be times when those outcomes are negative and you also need to take the same responsibility for them.

You might not even have been aware of the possibility of a negative outcome. You might have been played.

Despite your intelligence you just might have overlooked the potential negative outcome or miscalculated the risk. The reality is that we don't always get things right and we have to accept responsibility for our mistakes.

Your friends, family or colleagues might be dejected, disappointed, upset, angry. But these people are also human beings. They will have made mistakes themselves and will do so again in the future. The answer now is how you deal with it. The answer now is to take responsibility, fix what you can, accept, apologize and learn.

Standing strong, accepting responsibility and acknowledging it is tough. It's the hard thing to do. That's why so many shirk their responsibilities.

This is also about integrity. Do you have it? Are you prepared to own your integrity and take responsibility? In the long term this will pay off. Knowing that you're going take responsibility for your actions will make people trust and respect you more. They'll know that you're a person of integrity. They'll know that you're a person of your word. They'll know that you're a person that they want to be standing beside next time they make a mistake of their own.

Stand strong and tall, shoulders back. They were your actions, whether they were right or wrong, and you need to do the honorable thing and take responsibility for them.

The Power Of The Smile

Smile. Go on. Do it. Now.

How did it feel?

I tried it once. Obviously, I've smiled more than once, but I remember when I tried it as a strategy for the first time. I wasn't in the mood to smile but I forced myself to use my 43 facial muscles to smile. It was fantastic. My mood lifted. I felt better.

Despite my time on this planet I hadn't discovered this. Sure, I smiled a lot and was a positive person. But I hadn't realized that I could choose to smile when I didn't feel like smiling. The act of smiling would then lift my mood and even help me smile more. I could choose to be sad or I could choose to smile and be happier.

I'm not trying to share some amazing life-changing experience. I didn't develop some psychedelic high or anything crazy like that. But my mood ever so slightly improved. For the cost of just beaming a small smile the benefit of an uplift in mood is extremely worthwhile.

There are pages across the internet that will also tell you that it takes more of your facial muscles to frown than to smile. The truth is we're not all the same, we smile in different ways. There are different types of smiles and frowns and some of us even recruit a different number of facial muscles than others to form our unique smile. What's important is that smiling improves your mood. When you're down, angry, depressed, grumpy, obnoxious or irritable it will help lift you up.

Smiling isn't a miracle cure nor is it a prevention, but it can help. And the best part – it's free. You can smile any time you choose to.

Never go a day without smiling. No matter how hard it is, when life's really got you down, choose to smile.

Commit

I spent decades of my life failing to commit. That's not an exaggeration. I was flimsy. I flaked. My answers were maybes. "Are you coming to our wedding, to our party, to meet for a drink after work?" Maybe.

People couldn't plan. How do you do a seating plan for a wedding when someone is a 'maybe'? At other times I lost opportunities. They had to assume that my 'maybe', my lack of commitment, meant 'no'. I couldn't blame them. They had to get on with what they were doing and I couldn't confirm.

I was the 'maybe' man because I was scared. I was scared of committing. And the reason I was scared – in case a better opportunity came along. I didn't know what that better opportunity was or if there was any chance at all of it coming my way, but just in case, I said 'maybe'.

Maybe that better opportunity did come along. But maybe I missed it because the path to achieving it was lined by these smaller events. By giving my 'maybe' I had said no to the future opportunities that I was so desperately waiting for. By waiting for that better opportunity I ended up missing out on countless other opportunities that were right there. Some were just that wedding, that party, that drink. Others were huge opportunities which are created only by living life and seizing the smaller opportunities that I only gave a 'maybe' to.

Put yourself out there. Take the big leap by seizing the smaller opportunities. Be consistent and the bigger opportunities will open up from the smaller maybe-style opportunities. Earn the respect and trust from your friends, colleagues and acquaintances by being the committed 'yes' guy, not the 'maybe' guy. Don't spend your life wondering 'what-if', spend it knowing you did, you achieved, you seized, you committed. You might not realize it but it will open your life up to a whole new dimension.

Fear

$\mathcal{F}$ear consumes. It eats you up. It controls. It dominates. If you let it, fear can rule your life.

You can learn to take the upper hand. You can take back control. You can dominate that fear. You can use tactics and strategies to consume the fear inside you.

If you choose to take back that control and manage your fear it won't always be an easy path. Fear courses through our veins for a reason. Nature intended it to be there. To get rid of it entirely is near impossible and I'm not trying to promise you some amazing solution to eradicate fear completely. However, you can minimize your fears at appropriate opportunities and learn to work with them, to recognize them. You can harness that fear and work with it rather than working against it. You can remove some of the irrationality that fear brings out in us and apply rational wisdom as you source solutions to your immediate and longer-term problems.

Understand fear. Recognize it. Work with it.

The Dragon Won't Eat You

Dragons are scary. I remember as a child reading about them in books and watching them in cartoons and movies. They breathe fire. Often, they're the bad guy; standing in the way of the hero, defying justice and honor and the rule of law. They eat even the toughest warriors for breakfast.

I remember as a child fearing being eaten by a dragon. For a time, it was my worst fear. It was the worst thing that could possibly go wrong. It was the worst thing that could happen to me. My brain ticked over on this subject and I eventually came to the conclusion that I would have to avoid it. Cleverly, I thought at the age of about six, I had a strategy to avoid being eaten by a dragon. If I never went up against a dragon, if I never went head-to-head with one, then it would never be able to eat me. Easy.

Now, in adulthood, I find that many of us continue with this strategy. We avoid confrontation, stepping outside of our comfort zone, taking a risk or a gamble. It's easier not to take the chance. If we don't try it, if we don't go head-to-head with the dragon, then it won't eat us.

But what's the worst that can happen? Will someone not like your idea? Will someone shout at you? Will they think you're stupid? Will they eat you? I can pretty much guarantee that, if you take the gamble and go for it, all of these things will happen at some point with the exception of being eaten by a dragon. No one is going to eat you. Honestly. It just won't happen.

But there will also be times when your amazing idea will result in a pay rise, you'll be praised by your boss and they'll all remember how smart you are. At other times you might amaze your spouse or partner with your ingenuity. Maybe you'll astound yourself as you step outside of your own comfort zone or astonish the world as you invent the next Google.

Reach down deep inside and find the courage and commitment to go for it. Don't let that fear pin you down and prevent you from communicating your ideas and ambitions. The dragon won't really eat you.

Fear Exists In Your Head

Are you scared? Is it a rational fear? Often our fears aren't rational at all. Those that fear air travel will quite happily drive in cars and on roads that have a far higher statistical risk of serious injury or death.

Fear is all in your head. You choose to be scared, to be fearful. Of course, that's not strictly true. If your mind were free enough to choose then you probably wouldn't choose to be scared. But on a deeper level, one that may at first seem out of your control, it is you and it is your mind that is choosing to be scared and to feel fear. It is your own personal perception of the situation and how you choose to deal with it.

This means that as well as choosing to be scared, you can choose the opposite; you can choose not to be scared. You can decide to confront that fear head-on, to say no to it. It's up to you, it's your body, it's your mind, it's your choice.

It all starts in the brain, your brain. The hypothalamus portion of the brain controls the ancient survival reaction known as the fight-or-flight response. As your stress increases about 30 different hormones are released into the body, including adrenaline.

Confronting your fears and standing up to them can be one of the hardest things to do. In fact, just thinking about doing that probably invokes fear. The secret is not to reduce the response from the hypothalamus or the secretion of hormones – we might one day need these very real survival responses. The secret is to prevent the hypothalamus from being triggered in the first place.

Trying to prevent this trigger might seem a little impossible at first, but it works in stages. It starts by reducing the secretion of hormones and dealing with them before you can get close to full prevention.

Now for the hardest part - you need to choose to confront your fears. Pick just a tiny fear first. Step outside of your comfort zone and push your own boundaries. Don't think too much, just delve in and go for it. Force yourself to be scared.

Perhaps you're scared of picking up a spider or speaking to a random stranger. Stop what you're doing right now and go find that spider or a stranger. Commit.

How did it go? Did you die or suffer serious injury? No? OK, go and do it again. Right now. Then do it tomorrow and the next day.

How scared were you after a week compared to the first time? The fear will have reduced. The more you do this the more your irrational fears will reduce. And the best bit, this added confidence translates to your other fears. Your ability to manage other irrational fears and to cope under pressure will improve as you deal with these smaller fears.

Commit. Do it now. Step outside of your comfort zone and embrace a fear, whittle it down and conquer it. Choose not to be scared any longer.

It's OK To Be Scared

While fear is something that we've chosen, whether consciously or unconsciously, rational or irrational, the reality is that it's there. Fear exists in your head and we can take steps to reduce it and, often, eliminate it.

But, no matter how hard we try, fear will always exist somewhere. You'll never get rid of it entirely. That's reality. It's also a really healthy place to be. Fear helps to focus us, challenge us and excite us. It guides us in pursuit of our dreams and makes us question our own judgments and the sanity of our ideas. Fear helps make us humble, it helps make us human.

Managing fear can be critical to our success and I discussed how to do that earlier. Acknowledging that fear will not only still exist and that you'll be scared is critical too. It's ok to be scared.

The tough guy that thinks he's not scared of anything is the guy that just has too big an ego and lacks the intellect to understand fully his own cognitive processes. More likely he is scared but is too embarrassed and too scared to admit it. We're all scared of something and acknowledging those fears, recognizing and understanding them, provides our gateway to managing and embracing them.

Courage defines you when you're scared. It stands out as you dominate the fear. It empowers you to recognize that there is something else that is a higher priority to you than the restraint that fear imposes upon you.

Recognizing your fear, that you're scared, is a positive attribute allowing you to acknowledge when it's a healthy, rational fear and when it's not. And when you recognize that it's one of those irrational fears that we all have to deal with, know that it's just one more thing you need to overcome. Just one more obstacle that your courage will have to confront and battle, but that it's something you can choose to overcome.

Fear, being scared, is normal. Embrace it, don't hide from it. It's how you deal with it that counts.

Fear Of The Future

Do you spend your time wondering? Thinking 'what if'? Worried about your future, what it holds and how you can/should/could influence it?

You're not alone. Most of us do this. And, for most of us, we don't have the answers. Sometimes we think we do and we go for them. Sometimes we know we don't and we're stuck in limbo. Whether we have the answers and act on them or don't have the answers, there's one thing for certain: time keeps moving and you need to move with it.

That means you have to react. You have to decide. You have to commit.

Fear of the future, of your future, it a very real fear. No one wants to look back on life and regret it, thinking of the missed opportunities. You want to avoid that. That means:

** You need to decide what you want to do with your life.
** You need to decide what your goals are.
** You need to have a short, medium and long term plan and they need to link together.

Some of you reading this will know what you want to do, your goals and have detailed a 25-year plan. Most of you know that this stuff is a good idea but won't have it.

For those that don't have their plans in place, don't worry. Many of you won't know what you actually want to do in 10 years time. But, you've probably got a few ideas and a few things that you're considering.

Here's the reality. If you do nothing you will probably never achieve any of your options or possibilities that you're considering. You might never decisively know exactly what it is that you want to do in the future or where you want to be. But, if you don't pick something, commit and go for it, you'll be stuck in limbo.

You might pick the wrong thing. It's entirely possible. It might also be the right one. But if you don't pick you get none of them. And the chances are, along the way, you'll never get to where you planned to go anyway. Life changes. You will change. Your plan won't survive as you planned it and, often, it will change for the better. But without the plan, when you embark on your future path, there is no plan even to change.

You need to pick something. You need to proceed on the journey that it takes you along, full of drive and energy. You need to undertake that journey with commitment.

Take a minute. Consider your options. Commit. The only wrong answer is failing to commit. Whatever you pick, whichever journey you embark on, is the right answer.

Danger Perception

It's dangerous out there. Life is dangerous. Crossing the street, skateboarding in the park, commuting to work, leaping out of a plane or off a cliff, or participating in a variety of life's other adventures, challenges and battles. There's danger everywhere.

Fear is based on our perception of that danger. Actually, that danger is based on our perception. What one person perceives to be dangerous can be quite different to what another perceives. Of course, the ability to tolerate risk is a factor, but this is more about what the danger really is.

Science can put a number on any particular danger. But the real art is understanding that danger relative to you. It's often down to how you feel, your confidence and your knowledge of a particular danger. Your perception of danger, your willingness to tolerate risk will change each day and with your mood. The danger is what it is to you, not your parents, siblings, children or friends.

You can often reduce your perception of danger. Strategies include:

** **Training**. Practicing a skill relevant to the danger helps to reduce that danger. Learning to drive a car at an advanced level will reduce the danger to you and other road users.

** **Education**. Understanding the scientific principles behind a specific danger provides an avenue for the rational side of your brain to defeat the cognitive irrationality that we are prone to produce. This education aids our confidence and assists in reducing the perception of this danger.

** **Mitigation**. By mitigating the risks you reduce the danger and your perception of the worst possible outcome is lowered.

** **Elimination**. Eliminating the danger, or the threat of danger. This is often overlooked but is a simple concept.

** **Confidence**. With increased confidence, often aided by education (above), we're more prepared to see the rational and not give in to the irrational fears surrounding perceived danger rather than actual danger.

** **Mood**. Happy, positive confident moods allow us to be more tolerant and reduce our perception of danger. Conversely, lower moods fuel the danger perception fire. Make yourself smile, be happier and you're more likely to face that fear head on.

You can alter your perception of any danger. You can work with your fear and reduce it. Our response to danger is there for a reason but don't let it consume or overwhelm you. Think about it in advance, use strategies to face it and deal with it rationally.

Gratitude

*L*ife throws challenges at us. Sometimes it does this every day. Sometimes it does this on multiple occasions in a single day. It can be tough.

We can choose how we deal with these challenges. We can choose how we react to anything that's thrown at us, be it a challenge or an opportunity. We can even create our own opportunities. We can do all of this but it's how we go about doing it that really counts. Kindness, gratitude and grace are fundamental character traits that you can choose to emphasize and cultivate as you progress through life.

As you continue on your journey of life, consider how you really want to live and how you want to be remembered. Make the right choices.

Be Kind

There's a lot of hatred in life. In the western world we're subconsciously taught to fear and, as a result, hate. If you don't believe me just look at the newspapers – how many of their headlines and stories are designed to scare you? Politics is the same. The politicians invoke fear in us. They scare us with what will happen if we elect the wrong

41

politicians, turning us against other people, making us hate what the opposition stands for.

Hatred and fear are not the only answer. The alternative is kindness. It is not only the moral high ground, but it is where society should go. Just look at the tech-savvy bloggers on the internet. Many of them provide an abundance of material for free. Sure, they often want something in return but, largely, they understand the concept of karma. If they provide kindness they'll receive it in return. If they give away lots of free content you'll see the value and, perhaps, you'll click on an affiliate link or buy one of their products. Kindness works in both directions.

Kindness is the higher cause. Anyone can store hate or invoke fear. Use of it, to the extent that is becoming commonplace in western society, is unnecessary and immature. If that's all that me, you, the politicians or the media have as a weapon then our army just isn't strong enough and we deserve to lose the battle. Do we really need to stoop to that level consistently?

Avoiding the use of this hatred and fear isn't easy. I've used that tactic before and, like most other imperfect people, will end up doing so again. While I accept that refraining will be difficult, we can refrain and we can deploy an alternative weapon: kindness.

Kindness is often the moral high ground, the high ground where we do the right thing. It adds value elsewhere. But it can also be a selfish, yet justifiable, way forward. For me, when I'm kind, when I do a good deed, when I help someone out, I feel good. It makes me happy to make others happy. In a selfish way, being selfless actually helps you.

But for this selfish kindness to work it needs to be unreserved unapologetic kindness. Helping someone with the sole aim of getting that selfish endorphin reward doesn't work. You need to feel it genuinely. You need to believe whole-heartedly in helping them. You need to be sincerely and consciously kind.

Try it. Make it your goal. Every day. Not just once but repeat it. Sign up to deliver a Random Act Of Kindness. Every day help someone with something. It can be something small – helping someone to cross the road, slowing down to let a car out or putting some coins in a charity collection bucket – but do something. You'll quickly develop a habit. Without thinking you'll help others. It'll be instinct. Not only will those rewards come back to you at some point in the future but you'll feel those endorphins then and there.

Magnanimous in Victory

We all want to win. We want to succeed in our goals, in our battles, in our lives. That involves winning. If we're going to start something we want to come out the other side having been successful, having achieved, having won.

Sometimes winning means that someone else has to lose. Of course, there are times when you can both win and times when you can both compromise to provide a solution that isn't a huge loss. It's not as big a win for either side, but it's still a win.

Sometimes you need to be fair. You need to create and mold the situation to enable not just a win for your side but also for the other side. Why? Well there are two reasons:

** **An Out**. If you can give the other side, potentially your opponents, an out, a way to still win, then they're much more likely to take it, to back down, to concede.

** **The Long Term**. This isn't just about this battle, this success, this win. This is about the longer term. This isn't about this victory it's about your future victories. If you can, let the other side win too then they'll leave with a good experience and be prepared to work with you again in the future.

Your opposition, your opponents, need to have an out. You need to know this up front. If you want to win, don't make it their responsibility to find it, make it yours. If you can find their solution, you will find yours.

When it is in your power, be the stronger person by choosing not to crush your opponents. Choose the long term. Triumph in your victory yet remain magnanimous too. Let them exit with their dignity intact – next time they might just be on your side.

The Last Day

It happens to everyone. Sometimes you have warning, you know it's coming. More often you don't. You have your last day and that's it. Gone. All of a sudden that life is over. You can't get it back. It's gone.

It doesn't just happen to you but to all of us, to everyone. That means your friends and your family too. And what if that last day happened for them and you weren't there. Or you were there but you had an argument or a fight. Perhaps you just weren't the best person you could be that day.

It's not your fault. You weren't to know that it was their last day. But, then, perhaps you should have known. Perhaps you should have been prepared. Perhaps you should have considered the possibility that it could have been their last day and treated them accordingly.

What if, just in case, you treated everyone as if it was going to be their last day? What if you were overly pleasant and nice to them? You smiled, didn't interrupt, listened. You made sure their glass was filled and they got the meal they wanted. You were patient and caring. You shook hands when you arrived and hugged tightly when you left; a strong, thoughtful caring hug like it might be the last hug you ever gave.

And the bonus, what if it turns out it wasn't their last day. That they lived another and another day. Would you have lost anything? Would it have been worth it? Would you both have smiled with joy and treasured the memory of a beautiful time together?

Take it a step further. What if turned out not to be their last day but yours? You would have spent it spreading happiness and warmth to all those around you. Certainly not a bad way to go out at all.

Treat everyone as if today is his or her last day. It's a win win all round. You never know when it really will be and, if it's not, you'll be a happier more contented person.

Don't Be A Hater

When we're young we look up at life. We see opportunities, prospects, excitement. We wonder at what adulthood will provide for us. We look at photographs in magazines of distant places, we hear tales of adventures that others have had. We see a future that has the potential to be bright.

Then we age. We get older. Often, we realize that many of those opportunities won't be available to us. Perhaps we have friends that have undertaken some of these adventures or we read or hear of others who have visited one of these distant places that have been on our bucket list for years.

The lack of realization of our own dreams can slowly manifest itself in hatred. It can happen without you knowing it. It's not something that happens quickly, but a slow process that gradually eases into your life. Jealousy is often a catalyst here. The reality is that it's also a regret, annoyance of own failure to achieve and make these dreams, your own dreams, come true. Before you know it you're a hater.

A hater dismisses. A hater resents. A hater often harbors some form of jealousy. A hater, whether subconsciously or consciously, is fearful. A hater is not your friend.

The reality is that, if we're not realizing these opportunities, these dreams, then it's the life that we've chosen to live that is preventing us from realizing these opportunities. We're in the driving seats of own lives. No one else is. We're the ones in control. We're the ones who make the choices. Sure, there are people out there who add value to this process. There are others who subtract from it, get in the way and make it harder. These are life's battles.

Haters don't add value to these processes. They take away from it. Being a hater is miserable. Do you want to go through life with a smile on your face or a frown? Happy or unhappy?

You can choose to harbor hate and jealousy. You can choose to be positive and supportive. You can choose to smile or frown.

Avoid the haters. They're not your friends. Your friends are the people who add value, not take it. Don't be a hater yourself. Avoid the situations that might make you hate. Pick the right battles. Seize opportunities, take responsibility for your life's direction, work towards your dreams. Don't give yourself an excuse to be a hater.

Gracious In Defeat

Despite the battles we win, the preparation we undertake and the successes we accomplish the reality is that there will be losses along the way. We will fight battles and we will lose.

Perhaps you're a winner in life. Perhaps you don't lose. Perhaps you don't understand how this applies to you. That's fine. Skip this bit. But, maybe you're missing something. Perhaps, if you've never been defeated, and can never see yourself being defeated, you're fighting the wrong battles and staying seated too far within your own comfort zone.

For those of you who feel you're permanently winners, I know that there are countless arguments against this logic. I can already feel you on the defensive, feeling that need to defend yourself. But, what if I'm right? What if maybe, just maybe, there's a possibility that I'm right and you could be missing out on something?

Just maybe, the battles that you're fighting are too easy. I'm sure you put extra work and effort in to achieving your success. But there are probably other battles that you avoid because there's more risk. And maybe you just can't stand to lose.

But, perhaps it's OK to lose. I talk more about that in the Win The War lesson in Chapter 7. But, when we lose, we need to know how.

Grace is the only way. Losing with grace provides you with the opportunity to lose with dignity and humility. It's how you lose while retaining the highest level of self respect, and respect of your peers. It opens the possibility of you to remain in favor with your opponent and retaining as much good will as you can.

If you're living an honest life while pushing boundaries, dreaming, challenging yourself and smiling then you're going to lose the battle on more than one occasion. Know how to lose. Know how to lose with grace. Keep your dignity intact.

Know that it's a natural part of life's journey to lose, and to lose with grace.

Mindful

I'm busy. These days pretty much all of us are. The pace of life is fast. It's galloping along at an astounding speed and we need to keep up.

Keeping up means making time to slow down. It means taking the time to invest in ourselves. It means being mindful. Slowing down and investing in mindful activities will allow you to keep up. It will provide you with the tools to operate at an acceptable pace, if that's what you choose.

First off, you need to smile. You need to remember why you're doing what you're doing in the first place and enjoy life. For this to be possible, you're going to have to take those breaks, have downtime, and reflect. You will, at times, need to swallow your pride and step back, sometimes letting others in. In doing so you can believe in yourself.

Smile. Believe. Be mindful and experience a calmer, more fulfilling, more present life.

What Makes You Smile?

As a child I remember running around doing silly things. Sometimes I would be getting into mischief, sometimes I wouldn't. Simple things made me happy. Simple things made me smile.

As we grow older, as we mature, these same silly things make us smile less. Eventually, the responsibilities of life weigh heavier on our shoulders and our ability to have fun, to smile, diminishes further and we're left with a happiness flatline.

Studies show that, as we mature through different stages in life, we are less likely to experience the same highs that we used to. But, interestingly, it is often because we're less likely to push ourselves and put ourselves in the same situations that inspire us to experience those highs.

Of course, we still have fun, we still smile. I'm not suggesting that is taken away completely, more that we often seem to have lost our focus. It seems to take increasingly extreme measures to bring that once easily formed smile back to our faces.

Your happiness level is not purely hereditary. You control it. We all have a basal level of happiness from which we fluctuate and our daily ups and downs can elevate or reduce it temporarily from this baseline. As Shawn Achor demonstrates in his bestselling book The Happiness Advantage, habitually performing these daily activities that boost your positive emotions temporarily can, in actuality, permanently raise your happiness baseline.

What makes you smile? Ask yourself that question. Think hard. What's really there deep down inside you? Do you like to like to jump off cliffs, play with your dogs in the park, read romantic fiction or slaughter thousands of zombies on a video game? What makes you tick?

You need to know what really makes you happy. The small things all count. Sure, there are bigger picture issues that you need to consider in more detail like quality time with your family and close friends. But there's also 'you' time. The small things that make you smile each day. Don't let a day go by without indulging in one of those small things. Life is simply too short to see the sun set on a day that you didn't smile.

Work out what these small things are. They could be simple, they could be silly but they make you happy. Prioritize them. Make yourself happy. Make yourself smile. No one will do this for you. You need to choose yourself and you need to choose being someone that's happy and smiles.

So make a pact. Make a daily habit. Choose to smile and choose this every day.

Downtime

These 21st Century technologically enabled lives that this neo-modern era has forced upon us are jam-packed. Many of the tools that have been created to make our lives easier have become corrupted and, instead of making us more efficient, have increased our inefficiency. Email was meant to make us paperless and streamlined, yet most experiences result in a reality that is often a disruptive, time-consuming and only partially efficient system.

As businesses, customers and the government apply increasing pressures upon us and upon themselves to reduce friction and increase efficiency, productivity and ROI, flexibility is often reduced and pressures increased. It is now more important than ever to ensure you take effective downtime.

The more jam-packed your life, the more you need to ensure you take your break, breathe and reflect. Arianna Huffington's book *Thrive* covers this in detail. She shares her personal wake-up call after collapsing with exhaustion. She re-examines success in our ever-busy lives. "Today we often use deadlines – real and imaginary –to imprison ourselves," says Huffington.

No matter who you are, the harder you slave at whatever it is you do, the closer you risk burnout. No one is exempt. You can be the strongest, most resilient, most powerful individual but, without effective downtime, it will get you – it's just a matter of time.

Schedule time to pause, to recharge, to refresh. Make this a daily routine and a weekly routine. Take vacation. The real travesty with our bodies and minds is that we don't know that we needed a break until it's too late. Get ahead of the game and schedule in your own downtime.

Reflection

Downtime isn't the only thing we need to insert into our busy, modern day lifestyle. Reflection is a critical aspect if we want to take that next step in self-growth.

We need to reflect on our personal life plan, our business decisions, our direction, our considerations to our family's requirements, our forward projection and our strategic goals, amongst many other things. How else can we ensure that we've stayed on track, systematically veered from it and learned the lessons from our successes and failures?

We also need to compound further the information that we've gleaned and learned along this journey and ensure it remains present, filed in a cohesive form allowing the neurons and synapses to connect efficiently. Reflection aids this process as it contributes to the Spaced Interval Repetition (SIR) Technique.

SIR is based on the research of psychologist Hermann Ebbinghaus in the 19th Century. He discovered that we forget new information within a matter of minutes and hours unless it is presented to us again. Reflecting, at opportune moments, significantly increases retention; for example, reflecting on information after 1 hour, 1 day, 1 week and 1 month.

Leaders, at a variety of levels, have embraced the benefits of reflection. Perhaps it's scheduling in a 30-minute period at the start or end of each week to purposefully do so. Perhaps it's done during your commute home. Scheduling a time to reflect is the best way to make this happen.

As I struggle through the day, getting distracted, knowing that I'm not fully present or concentrating on the task in hand, I use reflection as a weapon. I note the subjects that are distracting me and write them down. I know that I have a period allocated later to reflect and will include them. This helps me clear my mind and become more focused. Of course, it's not always quite as simple as this; I'm not trying to suggest that reflection will suddenly make an imperfect life perfect again, but it's certainly a strong step in the right direction.

Reflection only works if you make time to do it. Schedule time to reflect, the more frequent the better, and do so on a regular basis. You'll think more strategically, become more present and improve your memory. Seriously, with these benefits, is there any reason not too?

Pride

There are people out there that are astonishingly smart. You probably know one or two. The ones that have this uncanny brain which is able to assimilate information at speeds infinitely quicker that you or I. I'm afraid that I'm not one of those people, most of us aren't.

But I have become an expert in certain niche areas in my professional life. I might not be the smartest person in the world but I've learned a great deal about these subjects. I've spent years understanding them. I've spent lots of my spare time reflecting on them, further improving my understanding as I cognitively process the information that I've gleaned.

I'm not the only one in the world to have done this. Pretty much every one of us has got good at something; experts in our own way. Yet there is so much more to be learned, to glean, to improve, to take that next step. Often, standing in our way, is pride.

Pride is a powerful phenomenon. It can be a powerful weapon and an even more powerful handicap. Our occasionally irrational brains often link it with our egos. To protect our egos we become too proud of what we've created, of our expertise, that we can become blinkered, failing to open ourselves up to a wealth of further possibilities. That is exactly what will hold you back. It's what will make you good but not great.

There's a place for pride yet you shouldn't be too proud to take advice. When I say take advice, I mean from every corner. I'm not just talking about taking advice from those better or greater than you. I'm talking about taking advice from anyone and everyone. Don't be too proud to ask those just starting out, your students, your employees, your subordinates.

Acknowledge that someone else might have a better idea than you or be better in a certain area. Even if something is 'yours' don't be scared to turn it on its head and have someone provide critical analysis or find potential areas to improve it, change it or even trash it.

Turn pride on its head. Use it to your advantage. In the long run, your ego will thank you, you'll improve and open up the possibility not just of good, but great.

Believe

Believe in your own abilities. It's simple; you must. I just wrote it down so you have to do it. If you don't believe in yourself how can you expect anyone else to believe in you?

The truth is, like many of us, I have negative thoughts and emotions and self-confidence crises. Most of us do. Those that don't are probably living too far inside their own self-comfort bubble to be really challenging themselves.

Just telling you to believe in yourself isn't going to cut it. I need you to do it and, I'm afraid, for those that struggle with this, I don't have a quick solution that will work after reading a page or two of a book.

However, I can point you in the right direction and arm you with tools as you battle the journey to belief enlightenment:

** **Start small**. What do you currently have that you believe in? It doesn't matter how small they are or limited. Dive deep and find them. Write them down.

** **Reaffirm these abilities**. Put your list on a wall, perhaps above your desk, the side of your mirror or next to your bed. Read them each day. Reaffirm your self-confidence by positively reinforcing them.

** **Take steps**. Build on the foundations that you've laid. Add more to your golf bag of confident abilities. Step outside of your own personal comfort zone – it's the only way. Go out on a limb and commit. What's the worst that could happen? Maybe someone laughs, but the rewards of new found confidence open up infinite possibilities. Take the chance.

** **Repeat**. Build on your list, continue to reaffirm it and then take small, actionable steps as you build your confidence higher and higher.

You'll be surprised that people will believe in you. It's amazing how quickly people can and will have confidence in you if they can see that you believe in yourself. Try it with something small that you know you can do and see the trust in people. As you expand your arsenal of self-confidence, others will follow in your own belief.

Stamina

$\mathcal{A}$s we journey through our ever-changing life we'll have some incredible experiences. Many will be positive experiences, but some will be negative. There will be highs and there will be lows. This is what happens as we travel down the road of life.

We have no choice. The journey continues whether we like it or not. The only constant in life is change. Holding on during the roller coaster ride can be tough at times. It takes stamina. We need to have the drive, guts and determination to keep going. When life is good, that's pretty easy. When life drops us down, it's harder.

Use the high times in your life to build your bridges. Replenish your memory banks with the good stories. The ones that make you realize exactly why you exist. The ones that empower you. You'll need them for when you crash down. All this will help strengthen your resolve and build your stamina up higher.

Arm yourself with more building blocks. Understand your weaknesses and how they can be converted to strengths. Fight for what's right but make sure you pick your battles to win the war. No matter what's happened before, drive forward. Make decisions. Take advice but act on what you believe, no matter how mad it might be. Above all, take action. You can have the best ideas and the best intentions in the world, but if you don't act on them, then they will all have been for nothing. Good luck.

Converting Your Weaknesses

We all have strengths. We can all excel. There are certain things that we're especially good at. Things that others can't do at the level we can or with the same speed and efficiency. Some of us have found these skills, these strengths, earlier than others.

Some people will read this and disagree. They'll think that they're distinctly average, or perhaps even below average. They'll think that they don't possess these skills or strengths in this way. In fact, some people will just see where they're failing. They'll see only their weaknesses.

The truth is, and I really believe this, that we do all have these strengths. Some people have just identified them earlier, that's all. Everyone has their unique way that they look at a specific area or problem. They can cast their personality onto it and add value in their own unique way; a way that no one else can.

But the real strength that we need to understand and harness is that of our weaknesses. We need to identify our weaknesses, at least the dominant ones, the ones that potentially hold us back the most. These are the weaknesses that we're most conscious of. They might, in all actuality, be small or others might not notice them. Conversely, to you, they might be overwhelmingly dominating. But right now they're your weaknesses.

Recognizing that we have weaknesses and identifying them specifically are the first steps. You can now work with them, manage them and provide focus in areas where you have strengths, not weaknesses.

Anyone can avoid his or her weaknesses – I've been doing it for decades. The real magic is in taking the next step. The real magic is in taking those weaknesses you have identified and turning them into strengths. The energy in those weaknesses is strong and can be harnessed.

Every weakness has a corresponding strength. List your dominant weaknesses and analyze them. What are the positive aspects of the characteristic that you are classing as a weakness? If you're arrogant then you're self-confident, if you're disorganized then you're creative, if you're emotionless then you're calm. Harness those strengths; don't dwell on them as weaknesses

Turn your weaknesses into strengths. Recognize and identify your weaknesses and develop your own strategy to stand strong. Your weaknesses can be your strengths, but only if you choose to make them so.

Fight

Fighting is important. It should be taught in school. There should be a whole class devoted to it. This is skill that you should learn as a child. It's a life skill, a life lesson that is one of those developing skills that forms our foundation.

Fighting takes confidence, guts, a nimble mind, style, strategy and perhaps a certain amount of panache. It can be calculated. It can be reactionary. It's tough. Often there's a winner and loser; there's certainly a risk of failure.

I'm not saying go out and pick fights, cause havoc, wreak chaos, incite riots or slaughter the innocent. I'm not talking about violence. I'm saying stand up for yourself. If you're not content, or in agreement, then say so. Don't idly go with the flow for an easy life. Stand strong and voice your opinion.

Having opinions and beliefs are a good thing. Stand behind them. Fight for them. Some will disagree. There will be haters. There will really be haters. There will be people that strongly disagree with you and hate what you stand for. They'll be vocal. They'll want to fight you. Don't let them put you off. At the same time there will be people that will agree with you, that will be on your side.

Don't give in to the haters. If they are genuine and fair fighters, listen to them - always be open to the possibility that you could be wrong or that there may be another answer - it will make you stronger and add strength to your position. If they're just examples of those horrible people in life then just ignore them, move on. Don't waste your time on them.

Stand up. Fight your corner. Have the courage of your convictions, of your beliefs, stand up for them, get behind them and be prepared to fight for them.

Win The War

It's a war out there. The whole world. We're at war. In our life, it's a war. You have to win it. You have no choice.

Winning the war is a long game. It won't happen today, tomorrow or even next year. Winning the war takes your lifetime. They'll be times when you think you've won, when you're up, and then someone comes out of nowhere and out flanks you.

Set backs are all part of it. They'll be times when you feel like you're losing. But it's a long game. It lasts your lifetime.

In this war of life they'll be many, many battles. Some you'll win, some you'll lose. Sometimes you'll choose not to even send your troops to the battlefield, accepting defeat without even crossing the start line. This is the art of your personal world war- deciding which battles to fight.

You can't fight them all. Some of them you'll be particularly passionate about. Some will have really riled you up. You'll be itching to pull your big guns out and use your complete arsenal of overwhelming force, deploying everything you've got.

Yet sometimes we need to step back, breathe, and understand our strategy. How does this short-term battle impact our longer-term war? Is it important? Is it a good use of your time and resources? On many of your most passionate cases, the answer will be no.

Of course, fighting and standing up for what you believe in is important. But to win that fight, that battle, we need to play the long game.

Take that breath and decide. Is this really a battle you need to fight on your journey to win your personal world war?

Don't Let The Past Hold You Back

Have you ever been told you're not old enough, don't have enough experience, don't have the right qualifications? Have you been prevented from doing something because of your past?

It happens all the time. We get judged on our past performances. The first thing that happens when you apply for a regular job is to submit your resume. They're looking at your past performance and judging you on that.

Are you going to let that hold you back? Not everyone of the same age is the same. Perhaps you're younger but more capable than someone much older. Experience counts but it's not everything. It's the same with qualifications.

In this cut throat world with fast hiring decisions required, judging people on their past performances is the easy way to sift through candidates. You can let this hold you back or you can do something about it.

I don't have a magical cure for you. I don't have a way you can circumvent employers and immediately land the job. But I can tell you that there are alternatives.

Jack Andraka was too young, had no qualifications and certainly had no experience. Yet, at the age of 15 he defied the R&D departments of the major pharmaceutical companies. He developed a test for pancreatic cancer that is 28 times faster, 26,000 times less expensive and over 100 times more sensitive than the current diagnostic tests.

Jack didn't dwell on his past. When 199 proposal letters he'd written to request assistance with his research on this 'hobby' failed, he didn't give up. Letter 200 struck home.

Jack's invention is saving lives. By not dwelling on his past, by focusing on what he can do, on his goals he's changing the World. You can too.

Don't sit in the confinement of your personal history. Get out there and create. Don't take no for an answer – find alternatives, persevere, succeed.

You can define history if you choose to. The past is the past, now drive forward and define the future.

Be Mad

"For an idea that does not first seem insane, there is no hope".
Albert Einstein

Do you ever have those crazy ideas? The ones that take courage to share with your family and friends and, when you do, they tell you that you're mad and that you shouldn't do them.

Having a sounding board, often made up of family or friends, is important. They can help you sort out the sometimes seemingly insane nature of your wild idea generating brain. This is very useful. We get to save embarrassment and only progress ideas that will actually work, saving an abundance of time, money and resources. Having that sounding board from our friends and family is a good thing.

But not all the time.

Sometimes they get it wrong. Sometimes the best idea is the one that everyone says is crazy. Sometimes the best idea is the one that everyone says no to. Sometimes the best idea is the craziest of them all.

If someone had told you they wanted to start a blogging service where people could only type 140 characters, would you have backed them? Hello Twitter (and, by the way, this wasn't even how it originally started). If someone had told you that instead of using horses they wanted to spend a fortunate building a mechanical contraption with wheels and an engine that ran on fuel from the ground would you think they were mad? And what about Alexander Graham Bell? His idea for a telephone was laughed at and look where we are now.

Sometimes your friends and family do get it wrong. Sometimes you need take the craziest idea of all and run with. Sometimes you'll be wrong but, sometimes, you'll be right.

Have the courage to listen to others, respect their advice and opinion but then make your own mind up. Commit. Make it happen. Be prepared to be mad; it's perfect madness after all.

Take Action

You can read this book, from cover to cover, all you like. Some of you will read it two, three or even four times. Some parts you'll agree with, others you won't. Different parts will hit different people in different ways. There will be "Ah-ha" moments.

But it's what you do afterwards that counts. The harsh reality is that the majority of readers won't take action.

Sure, you'll plan to. You'll believe you're going to. But most just won't. Most readers will nod in agreement with much of what I've written. They'll then sit back, have the intention to take action but never quite get around to it.

Taking action took a long time for me. I never quite got around to writing this book. I knew I had a number of books in me. I knew I had lessons and information that I wanted to share. I knew I wanted to write it but I never quite got around to making it happen. That's just one example of an array of times I never quite took action.

By reading this book you know, obviously, that I overcame that. The book is here and you're reading it. But it was tough. I had had the very honest intentions but never quite followed through. I had to admit my failures - not taking action. Admitting and accepting that failure was key to transitioning through the lack of action, avoiding the procrastination, taking responsibility, defeating the never ending excuses and just plain making it happen. No excuses – just do.

Be the person that stands out. Start small. Don't plan to write a whole book, defeat your worst fear or disrupt the largest industry. Write your first sentence, list a few fears or Google a few companies. The next day just build on it. Develop the small habit of taking action. Don't be the person in ten years time that didn't take action. Be the person that looks back with the accomplishments, failures and successes of the actions that you took.

Would You Like to Know More?

There's a lot more to learn - this is only Volume One. Stay up to date with my future books and follow the latest updates on my blog at http://www.PerfectMadness.com.

Don't forget the free offer that I made at the start of this book. I know that there are lots of different books that you could have purchased instead of this one. As a way of saying thank you for choosing this book I am giving away a free Toolkit. This Perfect Madness Toolkit provides you with everything you will need to live in the Perfect Madness frame of mind and is exclusive to my book and blog readers.

The journey that you are planning to embark on is not easy. Opening your mind to all the possibilities in the world can be exhausting. However, to ease your transition to an enlightened free spirit, I have carved many small steps into the mountain you will climb and provided a handrail as you navigate your new path.

You can download this toolkit directly by going here: http://www.PerfectMadness.com/Toolkit

Thank You

I want to say a final thank you for reading this book. You took a chance by picking this one and I'm confident you will feel you chose correctly. Many thanks indeed for buying this book and reading it to the end.

Now I'd like to ask just a small favor from you. Could you please take just a minute and leave a review for this book on Amazon. These reviews really make a big difference to me, my growth as a writer and to help others to find this book. The feedback will also help me to write more books and, of course, if you did love the content then please let me know.

Thank You.

CPSIA information can be obtained at www.ICGtesting.com
Printed in the USA
LVOW07s1336130115

422650LV00001B/11/P

9 780692 311165